INFO WISE

WRITE AND REVISE YOUR PROJECT

~Valerie Bodden~

Lerner Publications • Minneapolis

For Josh and our little projects—Hannah, Elijah, Titus, and Chloe

Copyright © 2015 by Lerner Publishing Group, Inc.

All rights reserved. International copyright secured. No part of this book may be reproduced, stored in a retrieval system, or transmitted in any form or by any means—electronic, mechanical, photocopying, recording, or otherwise—without the prior written permission of Lerner Publishing Group, Inc., except for the inclusion of brief quotations in an acknowledged review.

Lerner Publications Company
A division of Lerner Publishing Group, Inc.
241 First Avenue North
Minneapolis, MN 55401 USA

For reading levels and more information, look up this title at www.lernerbooks.com.

Main body text set in Adrianna Regular 11/18. Typeface provided by Chank.

The Cataloging-in-Publication Data for *Write and Revise Your Project* is on file at the Library of Congress.
      ISBN 978-1-4677-5225-1 (lib. bdg. : alk. paper)
      ISBN 978-1-4677-7582-3 (pbk.)
      ISBN 978-1-4677-6232-8 (EB pdf)

Manufactured in the United States of America
1 — CG —12/31/14

CONTENTS

WRITE ALL ABOUT IT

By this point in your school career, you've probably written lots of papers already, from "What I Did over Summer Vacation" to "Why My Cat Is the World's Best Pet." But perhaps you've never written a research paper. Have no fear! It's not as hard as it sounds.

Let's say you're off to a good start. You've already chosen a topic and done your research. You've found the best sources and taken notes on them. But now you're wondering how to turn those notes into a paper.

Like any paper, a research paper has a beginning, a middle, and an end. But unlike a paper based on your personal experiences, a research paper includes information from outside sources. And it gives credit to those sources through citations in the text. *What's a citation?* you ask. It's simply a note that lets readers know where you found your information. That way, your sources will get the credit they deserve and your readers will know you aren't just making things up.

A research paper has one more thing in common with any other paper: revision. After you've written your paper and cited your sources, you need to go back through it to make sure you've said everything in the best way possible. The result is a well-written project that makes its point clearly.

Give yourself plenty of time for each of these steps. Don't wait until the last minute and then rush to finish. So what are you waiting for? Let's get started!

CHAPTER 1

THE NECESSARY PARTS

Before you set pen to paper (or fingers to keyboard), take a moment to think about your purpose. Remember, a research paper isn't just a bunch of facts thrown together. It expresses your unique thoughts and ideas, supported by information and evidence from your sources. What is your thesis? Are you writing to explain, persuade, or compare?

Think about your audience too. Of course you are writing for your teacher, but who else might read your paper? Will your classmates see it? Maybe your family or other adults will read it.

Knowing *why* you are writing and *who* you are writing for will impact *what* you write. For example, if you are writing to explain black holes to your classmates, you should include explanations of technical terms that may be unfamiliar to them. If you are writing to persuade the school board to expand the band program, you might focus on how the program could improve the school's image in the community.

Once you have your purpose and audience in mind, pull out your outline—the blueprint or the map for your paper. You don't have an outline yet? No problem. You can write one now. Arrange your notes in a logical order that shows your paper's main ideas and the evidence you will use to support each point. Write down or type the gist of that information in a page or two. The outline doesn't have to be formal (unless your teacher requires it). But make sure that it gives you enough information to see where you are going.

You've done your researach and know all about black holes. But remember that your audience might be unfamiliar with black holes. Be sure to explain terms and scientific concepts when writing your paper.

If you follow your outline, the writing process should go smoothly. So keep the outline next to you as you write, and check in with it often—especially if you feel as if you're getting off track. Have you missed the point you were trying to make? Did you forget to add a key piece of evidence? Remember, though, that an outline is not set in stone. If, as you write, you find that part of the outline doesn't work, don't be afraid to change it!

THE BEGINNING

The first paragraph of your paper is the introduction. But it doesn't have to be the first paragraph you write. Some people find it easier to write the body of the paper first and then come back to write the introduction. If that works better for you, go for it!

No matter when you write the introduction, keep in mind that it's the first impression readers will have of your paper. That means it needs to snag their attention. There are several ways to do that. You can choose the one (or more) that works best for your topic.

You might start with an anecdote related to your topic. If you're writing about homelessness, for example, you might tell a true story of a teen who lived on the streets. Or you could begin with a surprising fact or statistic about your topic, such as this one: *The General Sherman, a giant redwood tree in California, is more than 2,000 years old.* You might also begin with a quote. Or you could show how the topic is relevant to readers' lives. For instance, you might begin a paper about the Amazon rain forest by explaining that the rain forest produces much of the oxygen in the air we breathe. In addition to grabbing the reader's attention, your introduction might provide a bit of background information on your topic. This can help your reader understand the issue and its importance.

No matter how you begin your introduction, the one thing it must include is your thesis. This is the sentence that states the point of your paper. It clues readers in about what you will explain or argue. You probably came up with a working thesis when you began your research. Make sure you decide on a final version before you start writing. Your thesis should be specific, and it should reflect your purpose. If you're writing about bullying, for

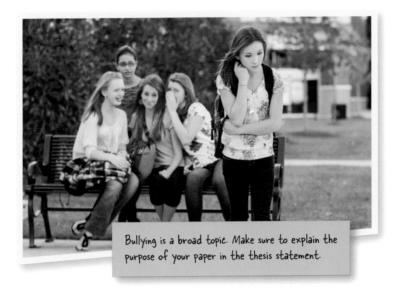

Bullying is a broad topic. Make sure to explain the purpose of your paper in the thesis statement.

example, your purpose might be to explain what bullying is. So your thesis might be this: *There are many types of bullying, including verbal bullying, social bullying, and physical bullying.* If, instead of just defining bullying, you want to offer solutions, your thesis might differ: *Parents, teachers, and students all have a role to play in solving the problem of bullying.*

THE MIDDLE

The middle of your paper is known as the body. This is where you prove your thesis. Depending on the length of your paper, the body will probably consist of two to four paragraphs. Each paragraph should focus on a different point. Say this is your thesis: *School uniforms save money, reduce teasing, and increase safety.* Your body might include one paragraph about how uniforms save money, another about how they reduce teasing, and a third about how uniforms increase safety.

Each paragraph should include a topic sentence. This is usually the first sentence of the paragraph, and it states the main idea of the paragraph. The rest of the paragraph supports the topic sentence with facts, examples, and other information from your sources. So for that school uniforms paper, the topic sentence for the first body paragraph might be this: *School uniforms save money.* Then the rest of the paragraph would show exactly how uniforms save money. Make sure to provide enough supporting evidence in each paragraph to prove your point.

As you write, try to make your ideas flow logically from one sentence to the next, as well as from one paragraph to the next. Your outline comes in handy here! You've already laid out a plan for the order of your paper. Now all you have to do is follow it. Adding transitions such as *in addition, besides, after, also, too, but, while, although,* and *finally* between sentences and paragraphs will help your writing flow more smoothly too.

THE END

Your final paragraph is the conclusion. Briefly summarize the points you've made in your paper and restate your thesis—in different words than you used in the introduction. You can also tell a final anecdote, use a powerful quote, or call on your reader to take action. Some of the most effective conclusions circle back to the introduction, reminding readers of an anecdote, a fact, or a quote introduced there. Remember, your conclusion is the reader's last impression of your paper. So make it strong and memorable!

PUTTING IT IN ORDER

There are many ways to arrange the body of your research paper. Which of these options will work best for your paper?

- **Chronological:** Arrange paragraphs in order of time, from what happened first to what happened last.
- **Simple to complex:** Present simple ideas first, followed by more complex thoughts so the reader can build an understanding of the topic.
- **Strongest to weakest:** Present the most compelling argument first, followed by increasingly weaker arguments. Or you could switch it around and present the weakest argument first, building up to the strongest.
- **Compare and contrast:** Discuss what is alike about two things and then what is different. Or describe all the qualities of one thing, followed by the qualities of the other.
- **Problem and solution:** First, present a problem, and then list one or more solutions.
- **Cause and effect:** Tell about causes that led to an effect, or describe an effect and then reveal what caused it.

CHAPTER 2

PROVING YOUR POINT

Imagine you're solving a crime. You know who the criminal is. But to prove it, you need to present and explain the evidence that links the criminal to his deed. Writing a research paper isn't much different. You're making a point by presenting and interpreting the information from your sources.

What kinds of evidence do you need to use? That depends. Let's look at a few forms of evidence you might incorporate into your paper:

Definitions

Use definitions to explain a process or a complex concept. Definitions tell what something is. For example, if your topic is green—or environmentally friendly—cars, you might first have to define what green energy is. Is it any form of energy that isn't coal or gas? Can it include fuels that still have some harmful effects on the environment? Do fuel-efficient cars count as "green" even if they use gas?

Narration

Narration is telling a story. Papers about a historical event might tell the story of how that event occurred. If you're examining cause and effect, you might also include narration in your evidence. Say you're writing

You might use a short narrative in the introduction to a historical research paper about the Oregon Trail.

about the Oregon Trail. You might include a true story about a person who traveled on the trail. Whenever you tell a story, keep it brief. And be sure to show how it is related to the point of your paper. Narratives often make strong introductions, as well.

Examples

Examples are specific instances that help prove or clarify a general statement. Examples can also help readers understand what you mean when you use an abstract term such as *heroism*. Do you mean risking one's life to save others? Do you mean working two jobs to provide for a family? Do you mean starting an anti-bullying program at school? Examples can also help explain a complicated fact or situation. Perhaps you're telling readers that tornadoes damage property. You can also say how many homes in a particular town were destroyed by a recent tornado. Examples do another important job: they make your writing more interesting. Sprinkle them in and watch your paper come to life!

Statistics

Statistics are numbers that present specific data. They can provide the hard facts you need to back up your point, but only if they are from a reliable source. The best way to ensure accuracy is to look for the same statistic in multiple sources. Do they agree? If not, you might include information from both sources and note the discrepancy. Also, be sure not to misuse statistics. For instance, if a statistic is based on information from one state, don't assume that it represents a trend in the entire country.

Are you researching Egyptian mummies? You can add credibility to your paper by quoting from experts who work in Egyptology.

Expert Opinions

Including expert opinions in your paper can boost your work's credibility. If someone in the know about your topic agrees with what you have to say, readers will be more likely to believe you. Be sure to mention your expert's credentials—for instance, instead of saying *Joann Fletcher believes there could be two-thousand-year-old Egyptian mummies buried in England,* you might say *Egyptologist Joann Fletcher of the University of York believes there could be two-thousand-year-old Egyptian mummies buried in England.* That way, readers can judge for themselves whether she is an authority on the topic.

Opposition

Especially in a persuasive paper, it is important to include the opposing viewpoint. Chances are that your readers know at least some of the arguments against your point of view anyway. If you ignore these arguments, they might think you are clueless—or, worse, dishonest. So present the opposing viewpoint. But then offer arguments to refute that viewpoint. Suppose you're writing about schools that require students to complete volunteer service for graduation, and you oppose the idea. You might write that those in favor of required volunteerism see it as a chance to teach kids about the importance of giving back. But then you can add your argument: students who are required to volunteer aren't doing so in order to give back but to get something for themselves. If you can't refute a point, admit it—but then show why your argument is strong in spite of this point.

You may be writing a persuasive paper that argues against a rule or a policy—such as required volunteering for students. Be sure to address opposing viewpoints in your paper.

In most paragraphs of your paper, you will use at least two—and probably more—of these types of evidence. And that's good. The more types of evidence you can provide, the more likely you are to prove your point.

USING YOUR EVIDENCE

So you know what kinds of evidence to use, but how should you incorporate that evidence into your paper? Should you use another author's exact words? Should you rewrite what your source says in your own words? Should you summarize a source's main ideas? The answer to all three questions is yes. Usually you will use a combination of quotes, paraphrases, and summaries as you present your evidence. So let's talk about how—and when—to use each.

When you quote, you use another person's exact words and you put those words in quotation marks so your reader will know they are not your own. It might seem easiest to always quote

your sources. That way you don't have to worry about paraphrasing their words or accidentally misrepresenting their ideas. Just remember, quotes are like seasoning. You want to use them to add flavor to your paper. But too many will overwhelm your paper. You can't rely on quotes to make your argument for you. You have to leave room for other information and your own interpretations.

Consider using a quote when your source phrases something uniquely or particularly well. Or quote primary sources such as novels, speeches, and autobiographies to preserve the original language. You might also quote an expert in the field to lend credibility to your argument. Or you might quote someone who holds an opposing viewpoint so that you don't risk misrepresenting the source's opinion.

In general, keep your quotes short, to convey just the essential information. You can include short quotes right in the flow of your paragraph. But if you use a quote that runs longer than four lines, set it apart from the rest of your text. Instead of using quotation marks, indent the entire quote and start it on a new line. It should look like this:

The stakes were high at the dig site. As a result, tensions were high too. As archaeologist Fantasia Notreal put it,

> I didn't come here to make friends. I came here to find dinosaur bones. This part of the country is packed solid with undiscovered fossils. It's the biggest Triassic burial ground we know about. Plenty of archaeologists want a piece of it. We have one year to make as much progress as we can. My advice is to dig in or go home.

Use long quotes sparingly, though. Your readers want to read *your* words and *your* ideas. Before adding a long quote, consider whether you could get the point across just as well by paraphrasing or summarizing.

Speaking of paraphrasing, that's what you do when you want to include your source's ideas or viewpoints but not necessarily the exact words. Paraphrasing means that you rewrite a specific idea from the source in your own words. When you paraphrase, don't just change a few words or rearrange the parts of the sentence. Instead, rewrite the entire idea without looking at your source.

Sometimes you don't need to quote or paraphrase. Instead, you might just summarize a source. That means you're not just restating one particular idea from a source. You're reflecting the overall point of a paragraph, a chapter, or even an entire work. This is useful when you want to mention background information or present an overview of an expert's opinion on a topic but don't need to go into detail.

A MATTER OF INTERPRETATION

Evidence is great, but it can't prove your point for you. You have to interpret and analyze your evidence for your readers so they can understand its significance. Say you wrote, *Nearly a quarter of the bee population in the United States died off during the winter of 2014.* So what? Is that more bees than usually die off during the winter? Is it a problem that part of the bee population died off? In other words, what does this mean, and why is it significant? You need to add a sentence before or after (or before *and* after) the evidence to help the reader interpret this fact.

Here's an example: *Bees continue to die off in record numbers. The winter of 2014 claimed nearly one-quarter of all bee colonies in the United States. Bees are needed to pollinate most of the country's food crops, so high die-off rates could lead to serious problems in the nation's food supply.* Now your reader knows the significance of the bee die-offs.

When you are writing an informative paper, keep your interpretation objective, or neutral. Explain the facts, but avoid using labels such as "good" or "bad"—and other words and phrases that express your personal feelings. Consider these examples: *Unfortunately, soccer is not one of the United States' most popular sports.* Or, *A fantastic new technology can help autistic children communicate.* In an informative paper, it's not your job to make judgments like these. Your job is to help readers understand the facts so they can make their own judgments. So ditch words such as *unfortunately* and *fantastic.* Let your readers decide what to think once they understand the facts.

If you're writing a persuasive paper, on the other hand, you do need to make judgments—and you need to back them up. How do you think a problem should be solved? Which prediction or theory do you believe is right? This is where another level of interpretation comes in. You have to explain your view of the facts. And you have to show how those facts support your own opinion.

Your research shows that thousands of books were banned from schools and libraries in a ten-year period. How will you interpret this data for your argument?

For instance, say you write this: *From 2000 to 2009, people attempted to ban more than five thousand books from schools and libraries across the United States.* First, to help the reader understand this information, you might discuss whether this is more or fewer books than have been challenged in the past. But you also need to explain what you think about this information. Do you view the number of book challenges in a positive light—as a sign that parents and other concerned citizens want to protect young people? Do you think more books should have been challenged? Or do you view these challenges in a negative light—as an unfair limit on what young people are allowed to read and think about? Do you think far fewer books should be challenged? Do you think no challenges should happen? Without interpretation, readers won't know which view of the topic you take. And you won't be able to persuade them to agree with you.

No matter what kind of paper you are writing, make sure that the evidence says what you are saying it says. Don't twist it to fit your purposes. Not only is that unethical, but it's also a red flag to your readers. If readers can't trust your interpretation of your evidence, they probably won't trust the rest of your paper either.

CHANGING QUOTES

When you quote, you can include the original source's sentence in full or you can use just parts of it. You can leave out some words by using an ellipsis (three periods) to show the omission. If you need to, you can change the tense of a word to make it better fit the grammar of your sentence. Just place the changed word in brackets. You can use brackets to add a brief explanation of a complex or unfamiliar term too. Just remember, no matter what you add or delete, you need to preserve the author's meaning.

Check out these techniques in action: *According to journalist Guy Wemadeup, the school is "finding it difficult to get enough funding [money] for a skydiving team" even though "it's clear the student body . . . is in favor of it."* The imaginary journalist quoted here used a term that readers might not know, so the bracketed word explains it. He also probably talked about something that wasn't directly relevant, so his statement was shortened with ellipses.

CHAPTER 3

CITING YOUR SOURCES

As you're adding evidence into your paper, you need to let readers know where you got the information. You need to cite your sources. *Why?* you ask. *Shouldn't readers assume that since this is a research paper, the information in it comes from my research?* Sure, maybe. But they won't know which information is taken from your sources and which is taken from your own head. And they won't know which facts come from which sources. And think of all the work the authors of your sources put into researching and writing their books or articles or websites. You need to give them credit for that work.

In addition, citing your sources adds credibility to your paper. Say your friend tells you that the average temperature on Pluto is -400°F (-240°C)? Do you believe him? What if he tells you he got this information from the NASA website?

Are you more likely to believe him? It works the same way when you cite your sources. If readers know your information is from a reliable source, they will be more likely to trust it—and to trust that you have done your job in putting your facts together. And if they want to know more about your topic, citations allow them to go straight to the source.

PLAGIARISM

One of the most important reasons to cite your sources is to avoid committing plagiarism. You probably already know that plagiarism involves taking credit for someone else's work. You wouldn't turn in a paper written by someone else and claim it as your own. But perhaps you didn't realize that failing to cite your sources is plagiarism as well. So is forgetting to place quotation marks around a direct quote, even if you do cite the source. Paraphrasing your source too closely is plagiarism too. A reader could easily assume the source's words are yours.

Often these types of plagiarism occur by accident. You might have forgotten to cite your source in your notes, so you think the idea must have been your own. Or you might be having such a good time writing that you don't want to interrupt your flow by stopping to insert citations. Even if you fail to cite a source by accident, you're still guilty of plagiarism. And plagiarism isn't just an ethical problem—it's also illegal. An author's work is legally protected by copyright. So the costs of plagiarizing can be severe. As a student, you'd be looking at a failing grade. For an adult, consequences range from a monetary penalty to the loss of a career.

WHAT TO CITE

Here's the good news: you can avoid plagiarism if you're careful. The first step is to take good notes, making sure to indicate the source for each idea and to put quotation marks around all direct quotes. If you're thinking, *Uh-oh, I didn't do that,* you need to go back to your sources to figure out where everything came from. It might sound like a lot of work—and it is—but it beats being accused of plagiarism.

Say you're past the point of taking notes, though, and you've done a good job with it. Congratulations! Next, you can take some steps as you write to keep your work plagiarism-free. The best way to avoid plagiarizing is to know *what* you need to cite and *how* to cite it.

Let's start with *what*. Basically, cite any information that is not your own. Obviously, when you use a quote, you are using someone else's ideas and even their words, so you need to cite that. But you need to cite paraphrases and summaries too. If you don't, readers will assume that these are your own ideas.

A good researcher takes careful notes while reading. Be sure to write the source name and use quotation marks when copying direct quotes.

The one exception to the cite-everything-that's-not-yours rule is that you do not need to cite common knowledge. That means you don't need a citation for facts most people already know, such as that water freezes at 32°F (0°C). Usually, these are the types of facts you know even before you begin researching your topic. If you're not sure if something is common knowledge, cite it just to be safe.

HOW TO CITE

Now you know *what* to cite. Your next challenge is *how* to cite. You've already put together a bibliography listing all the important information for each of your sources. But that bibliography will go at the back of your paper. It won't tell readers where you've used which sources in the text. That's why you also have to cite sources throughout your actual paper.

Your teachers will probably expect you to use parenthetical citations. Sounds scary! But it's not. A parenthetical citation is simply a citation that appears in parentheses within the text of your paper. Just to complicate things a little bit, though, parenthetical citations are not done in the same way for all papers. That's because there are many different styles for writing research papers, and each style follows slightly different rules. Two common styles are MLA style, the style of the Modern Language Association, and APA style, the style of the American Psychological Association. Your teacher will tell you which style to use.

Fortunately, the differences between MLA and APA citations are relatively minor. For MLA, include the author's last name in the citation, along with the page number from which the information came if it is a print source. You do not need any punctuation between the two items. For online sources, you don't need to worry about page numbers.

For APA, you still include the author's last name, but you follow that with the date of publication. Separate the two items with a comma. If you are citing a direct quote, add another comma after the date, followed by the abbreviation *p.* (for page) or *pp.* (for pages) and the page number. For paraphrases and summaries, page numbers are optional. Just remember that the more detailed your citation, the easier it will be for the reader to find the information in the original source. In either style, if no author is listed, use a shortened form of the work's title instead.

So if we were to cite this page of this book in each style, it would look like this:

MLA

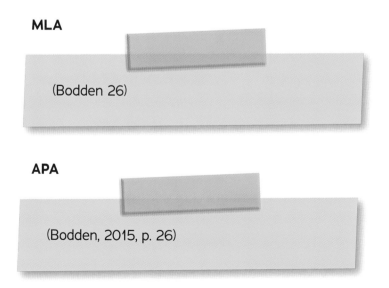

(Bodden 26)

APA

(Bodden, 2015, p. 26)

You probably have one more burning question: *Where do I put my citation?* Keep it as close as possible to the cited information. Usually, this means putting your citation at the end of the sentence containing the borrowed information. If you are quoting in APA style, place the citation immediately after the quote, even if it's in the middle of a sentence.

If several sentences are based on the same source, you do not need to add a citation after each sentence. You can place it after the last sentence from that source. Indicate where the borrowing begins by adding a statement at the beginning of the section such as, *According to Bodden . . .*

A parenthetical citation follows the last word of your sentence, before the period. If your citation follows a quote, the parentheses should be outside of the quotation mark but inside the period. Here's an example:

MLA

"A parenthetical citation follows the last word of your sentence, before the period" (Bodden 27).

APA

"A parenthetical citation follows the last word of your sentence, before the period" (Bodden, 2015, p. 27).

You can also incorporate the name of your source into your sentence. Then your MLA citation needs to contain only the page number. An APA citation would include the date immediately following the author's name and the page number at the end of the sentence, like this:

MLA

Bodden says, "You can also incorporate the name of your source into your sentence" (28).

APA

Bodden (2015) says, "You can also incorporate the name of your source into your sentence" (p. 28).

That's a lot to remember. But don't worry. There are entire books devoted to MLA and APA style. If you're stumped, grab a copy of the *MLA Handbook for Writers of Research Papers* or the *Publication Manual of the American Psychological Association.* Or check out an online guide. And if you still have questions, ask your teacher to go over the rules with you and to double-check a few of your citations before you officially hand in your paper. You'll be citing like a pro in no time!

PLAGIARISM AND THE INTERNET

In some ways, the Internet has made it easier than ever to commit plagiarism. After all, you can just highlight the text you want, copy it, and paste it into your document. And much of the information on the Internet is free to access. But that does not mean you can use it without acknowledging the source. Most online documents have the same copyright protections as print documents. So if you don't cite your online source, you're committing plagiarism. And while the Internet makes plagiarism easier to commit, it also makes it easier to catch. All your teacher has to do is enter the words of your paper into an online plagiarism checker to see if you copied them from an online source. So treat Internet sources just as you would any source, and cite them!

CHAPTER 4

REREAD, REVISE, AND REFLECT

Mission accomplished! You've written your paper, incorporated your evidence, and cited your sources. All you have to do is hand it in and wait for your teacher to give you an A+, right? Not quite yet. What you've written is the *first draft* of your paper. It's not ready to be handed in yet.

That's because your first draft is probably pretty rough. It might be missing arguments here and have irrelevant information there. Some points might be out of order, and you probably even have some typos. And that's fine! The whole point of a first draft is to get your ideas down. But now it's time to revise, to write a second draft and maybe a third draft and a fourth draft too—as many as it takes to get a great final product.

THE BIG PICTURE

If you have time, set your first draft aside for a day or two before you begin revisions. That way, when you come back to it, you can look at

it with fresh eyes. When you are ready to revise, you'll probably want to start by looking at the big picture. In other words, make sure that your paper does what it's supposed to do: supports your thesis.

As you read through each paragraph, think about how it proves your thesis. What does it add to your argument? Is there enough evidence to support each point? Have you introduced and interpreted the evidence to show its significance?

Don't despair if you identify weak paragraphs. Just go back to your notes to find more supporting information. If you can't find it there, go all the way back to your sources—or find some new sources—and do some more research. Then add a few sentences to support your point.

As you look at the big picture, you also need to consider whether your paper contains any irrelevant information. That's anything that isn't directly related to your thesis. For instance, you might think it's cool that George Washington's false teeth were made of ivory—not wood. But that fact isn't relevant to Washington's role in the American Revolution. After putting so much time and effort into researching your topic, it can be tempting to throw everything you've learned into your paper. After all, you want your teacher to know how hard you've worked. But irrelevant information only weakens your argument and confuses your reader. So delete it, no matter how great you think it sounds. You can always file it away for a future research paper.

Once you feel that your paper contains everything that should be there and nothing that shouldn't, read it again. Check the flow. Chances are, if you've been adding and cutting things, it might seem a little choppy. Now's the time to do some rearranging. Move sentences and paragraphs around so they flow logically from one idea to the next. Add transitions between ideas too.

DOUBLE-CHECK THE DETAILS

Once the big issues are dealt with, turn to the small stuff—punctuation, grammar, and spelling. Your computer can find obvious errors for you. But don't stop there. Read through your paper carefully, looking for places you may have missed commas or used one word (such as *there*) when you really meant another (such as *their*). Make sure your sentence structure varies throughout your paper. Do you have some long sentences and some short sentences? Do you have a mix of simple and compound sentences? Have you avoided starting several sentences in a row in the same way? Look at your word choices too. Could they be stronger or more precise?

USE YOUR FRIENDS

When you get close to your final draft, it can help to have a friend or a classmate read over your paper. Ask your reader to point out places where your arguments aren't clear or where there are unanswered questions. Have your reader look for awkward wording and typos too.

When your reader points out problems or gives you suggestions, don't be offended. After all, that's what you wanted him to do! Look carefully at the points your reader has made. Think about whether his suggestions might make your paper stronger. If they will, go ahead and incorporate them. But remember, it's still *your* paper. You don't have to make changes that you don't think will improve it.

Offer to review your reader's paper too. It's the polite thing to do if he's reading yours. And it can also teach you a lot. As you review the other paper, you may notice issues that you'd never thought of before. Does your friend begin every paragraph the same way? Hmmm. Maybe you should check if you do too. Did your friend write a particularly strong conclusion? Would your paper benefit from some similar techniques? Don't just wonder. When you get your paper back, go ahead and try it! Do a little final experimenting. And remember to thank your reader for the help.

The biggest reason to have a salad bar in the cafeteria is ~~because~~ *that* it is good for kids' health. Kids between 9 and 13 years old should have at least two cups of vegetables per day—and more if they exercise a lot ("How Many Vegetables Are Needed Daily or Weekly?" 1). Right now, our cafeteria has less than one cup of vegetables in most lunches. Those vegetable servings are almost never fresh vegetables (Perez 4-5). A salad bar would offer more options for kids. Some school officials doubt that kids will actually use a salad bar and say kids might actually ~~less~~ *Fewer* vegetables if it's up to them (Tarkington 2). But a survey of Haviland Middle School students showed that most students said they would use a salad bar. Kids would rather have fresh, tasty vegetables than the cooked, processed vegetable

like this year?
Explain what they really are
How many students?
What grades?

Ask a friend or a classmate to read the rough draft of your paper. That person should look for typos and places where your argument is unclear.

MAKE IT FINAL

You've read through your last draft, and you feel good about your paper. You're just about ready to turn it in. But first, make sure it is formatted according to your teacher's instructions. Are you supposed to use 1-inch (2.5-centimeter) margins? Should you double-space? Do you need a cover page? Paying attention to all those little details will show the time and care you put into your project.

Don't forget to add your finalized bibliography to the end of your paper too. Double-check that it lists all the sources you've

cited in your paper. Take off any sources that you ended up not using. Alphabetize the list by authors' last names. Be sure all your entries are written according to whichever style your teacher requested. Use a style manual for help if you need it.

And then you're done! Hand in that paper and pat yourself on the back.

TIME FOR REFLECTION

Now that your paper is finished, you probably don't even want to *think* about it for a while. But let's ponder the process one more time. It'll pay off down the road.

Think back to when you first started this project, before you even had a topic picked out. Think about the steps you followed to complete the assignment. How did you choose a topic? Did you do preliminary research? Which research techniques were most

WHAT'S THE POINT?

Maybe by this point you're asking yourself why you even need to write a research paper. After all, once you're done with school, you'll never need these skills again, right? Wrong! Research is a skill you'll use in nearly any career. And in many fields, you'll have to write about your research. Lawyers, doctors, journalists, politicians, scientists, engineers, librarians, and even video game developers need to know how to transform their research into written documents. So the practice you're getting with research can only benefit you in the future!

successful for you? Once you found your sources, how did you figure out which ones were relevant and credible? Did you use some sources you wish you hadn't used? Or did you miss sources that you wish you'd found earlier? Which sources were the most valuable?

What about note-taking? Did you use index cards, a notebook, or a computer? How did you label your notes to indicate their sources as well as the topic of each note? Did you arrange your notes into an outline before you started writing? How did the writing go? Did you follow your outline? How much revision did you need to do? Did you give yourself enough time to finish before the due date?

As you think about these questions, make some notes for yourself about what worked well and what you would have done differently. Maybe you wish you had spent more time looking for sources before beginning to take notes. Or maybe your outline was so detailed that the writing stage flowed quickly and smoothly.

Thinking about this now—not next week after you've forgotten all about this project—will help you the next time you have to do a research paper. And, yes, there will be a next time. There will probably be *many* next times. But you'll know what worked for you and what didn't, and what to do the same way next time and what to change. That will make the whole process easier. You might even have some fun. But for now, give yourself a pat on the back and celebrate: you've written a research paper!

NOW YOU DO IT

Let's get some practice incorporating evidence into a research paper. Look up your favorite athlete or musician in a book or online. Try to find three different types of evidence to show why this person is so great. You might find an example of a great play she made. Or you might find statistics about the number of albums he has sold. Maybe you'll find a striking quote about this person. Once you've found the evidence, write a paragraph that incorporates it. You can quote, paraphrase, or summarize, but be sure to introduce your evidence and interpret its significance for your reader. Cite each source using MLA or APA style. When you are done, read through your paragraph. Add transitions to make it flow well.

GLOSSARY

anecdote: a brief, often entertaining, true story

bibliography: a list of sources used in preparing a research project

chronological: ordered from earliest to latest or more recent

copyright: the exclusive legal right of the creator of a work of art or literature to produce, publish, or sell his work

credentials: evidence that a person is qualified for a specific position or level of authority

credibility: the quality of being believable or trustworthy

discrepancy: a disagreement or difference

paraphrase: restating someone else's words or ideas in your own words

persuade: to convince someone that a certain viewpoint is correct or to take a certain action

preliminary: an early stage of a project

primary source: a source that is written or recorded at the time of an event and reveals firsthand information about the event. Primary sources include autobiographies, letters, and news accounts.

refute: to prove someone or something wrong

transition: a word or phrase that connects two ideas

unethical: not morally right

SELECTED BIBLIOGRAPHY

Ballenger, Bruce. *The Curious Researcher: A Guide to Writing Research Papers.* New York: Pearson Longman, 2004.

Chin, Beverly Ann, ed. *How to Write a Great Research Paper.* San Francisco: John Wiley & Sons, 2004.

Lannon, John M. *The Writing Process: A Concise Rhetoric, Reader, and Handbook.* New York: Pearson Longman, 2004.

Lester, James D., Jr., and James D. Lester Sr. *Research Paper Handbook.* Tucson, AZ: Good Year Books, 2005.

Turabian, Kate. *A Manual for Writers of Research Papers, Theses, and Dissertations.* Chicago: University of Chicago Press, 2013.

Wolaver, A. "Tips on Writing a Persuasive Paper." Bucknell University. May 18, 2014. http://www.facstaff.bucknell.edu /awolaver/term1.htm.

FURTHER INFORMATION

Bodden, Valerie. *Research and Synthesize Your Facts*. Minneapolis: Lerner Publications, 2015.

Still stuck at the note-taking and outlining stage? Get tips and pointers on how to get the information you need from your sources.

Persuasion Map

http://www.readwritethink.org/files/resources/interactives/persuasion_map

This site can help you map out the arguments and evidence you will use to support your thesis.

Purdue University Online Writing Lab

https://owl.english.purdue.edu/owl/section/2

Got a question about how to cite a source? Check out this writing lab for guidelines in both MLA and APA style.

Scholastic Writing Workshop: Research Paper

http://teacher.scholastic.com/activities/writing/minilessons.asp?topic=Research

Get an overview of the steps needed to write and revise a research paper, as well as printable worksheets to help you draft and edit your paper.

Time for Kids: Writing Tips

http://www.timeforkids.com/homework-helper/writing-tips

Get tips for researching and writing your paper from writers at *Time for Kids.*

INDEX

PHOTO ACKNOWLEDGMENTS

The images in this book are used with the permission of: © Katerinache/Dreamstime.com, p. 4 (top); © iStockphoto.com/sd619, p. 4 (bottom); © iStockphoto.com/CamAbs, p. 5; © iStockphoto.com/deepblue4you, p. 6; NASA/JPL-Caltech, p. 7; © iStockphoto.com/AfricaImages, p. 8; © Kevin Dodge/Blend Images/Getty Images, p. 9; © Monkey Business Images/Shutterstock.com, p. 10; © Zoonar/Thinkstock, p. 12; © iStockphoto.com/milehightraveler, p. 13 (top); © iStockphoto.com/andreusK, p. 13 (bottom); © Peter Spirer/Dreamstime.com, p. 14; © Alistair Berg/Iconica/Getty Images, p. 15; © iStockphoto.com/DNY59, p. 16; © iStockphoto.com/herraez, p. 17; © iStockphoto.com/tr3gi, p. 18; © iStockphoto.com/CEFutcher, p. 19; © Mike2focus/Dreamstime.com, p. 20; © John R. Foster/Science Source, p. 22; © iStockphoto.com/Maica, p. 24; © iStockphoto.com/arissanjaya, p. 25; © Hero Images/Getty Images, p. 29 (bottom); © iStockphoto.com/tombaky, p. 29 (top arrow); © iStockphoto.com/spxChrome, p. 30; AP Photo/Gerry Broome, p. 31; © Digital Vision/Getty Images, p. 32; © Todd Strand/Independent Picture Service, p. 33; © Tetra Images/Getty Images, p. 34.

Cover and interior backgrounds: © koosen/Shutterstock (brown background); © Mrs. Opossum/Shutterstock (zigzag pattern); © AKSANA SHUM/Shutterstock (diamond pattern); © AtthameeNi/Shutterstock (blue-lined graph paper); © Looper/Shutterstock (arrows); © AlexanderZam/Shutterstock (graph paper dots); © oleschwander/Shutterstock (yellow lined paper dots).